The Grea

Agenda 21: The NW Exposed!

Food Crisis – Economic Collapse – Fuel Shortage – Hyperinflation

MW01076714

Rebel Press Media

Disclaimer

Our other books

Check out our other books for other unreported news, exposed facts and debunked truths, and more.

Join the exclusive Rebel Press Media Circle!

You will get a new updates about the unreported reality delivered in your inbox every Friday.

Sign up here today:

https://campsite.bio/rebelpressmedia

Introduction

Real inflation already 13% if fairer calculation method to 1980s is followed - 'G7-EU underline with choices that they themselves are an existential problem, not the solution'

The main Western nations have finally selected a route that is killing both our economy and our democracy and prosperity at the G7+1 (EU) conference in England. According to the London Financial Times, which openly advocates the communist 'Great Reset,' Joe Biden has gained backing for his plan to continue spending massive sums of money. This would be done to prevent the population's 'inequality' from worsening - an inequality that these self-styled elitists have not only created for themselves, but which threatens to worsen as a result of their policies.

The G7+1 leaders and their partners visited the Eden Project on Friday evening, where they met Queen Elizabeth and other members of the royal family. The Eden Project is a depiction of the "green" earth in the future. Every year, around 1 million people visit the domed botanical gardens. Sr. Tim Smit, co-founder, remarked that Eden's "goal is for the world to acquire its energy from renewable sources."

This is on par with the so-called carbon-neutral society that the West wishes to establish at exorbitant cost (but which can only be realized by forcibly lowering citizens' energy usage - and thus their wealth and freedom).

Low interest rates combined with unrestricted spending equals financial economy collapse.

Prime Minister Mario Draghi, the former president of the ECB who wiped out the (government) bond market in 2014 by introducing negative interest rates - which, by the way, failed - was, of course, a great advocate of a "expanding fiscal policy," i.e., cranking up the money presses even more, which is causing the first tangible signs of screaming inflation in the US (Simply compare your weekly shop transaction to one or two years ago).

'With artificially low interest rates, they have devastated the banking economy,' claims Martin Armstrong, an independent American economist. 'This means they will no longer be able to borrow indefinitely.' As a result, they have accepted Modern Monetary Theory (MMT), arguing that they can now simply keep printing money indefinitely, and any inflation is purely transient as a result of Covid's deficits.'

'Real inflation is already 13%,' and for beef, it's even 20% to 30%.

The Federal Reserve of the United States is likewise on board, maintaining ultra-low interest rates and purchasing (government) bonds. Although the 'Fed' concedes that inflation is already 'higher than expected' - up to 5% (vs. 1.4%) in 2020, the highest level since the 2008 financial crisis - it sees no reason to interfere. According to'shadowstats.com,' true inflation is already above 8%, and might be as high as 13% if it were still computed the old-fashioned method (1980s). However, in the West, the calculating methodologies have been purposefully modified in order to report the lowest possible inflation.

The many-fold increase in real inflation is now having an effect on citizens. According to a meat dealer, the true rate for meat goods is closer to 20% to 30%, but the media continues to publish "just" 10%. CBS News spoke with an average Maryland shopper who claimed she already spends $150 on groceries each week, which is more than double what was common just a few years ago.

Purchasing power is eroding at an unprecedented rate; 'the economy will be in far worse position in six months.'

The purchasing power of the dollar has not fallen this much since 1982, and this is a direct result of the government's inflationary policies. This has now resulted in a record drop in the index of anticipated housing and car purchases. More and more people are just spending too much money on groceries, rent/mortgages, energy, and transportation to afford any new purchases. Meanwhile, large investors, who have already purchased almost a quarter of all residences in the fashionable Houston area, are artificially driving up housing prices considerably (20 percent of the houses remain empty after that).

'And for those who are thinking, but our wages are going up as well, I have only one piece of bad news: all support measures will end in September,' says firm Zero Hedge analyst Tyler Durden. 'Just wait until October, when everything changes...' All those manufacturers and sellers who have grown accustomed to stronger demand and considerably higher pricing will have to face a difficult choice: either significantly lower prices again, or sell fewer items and services... One thing is certain: the US economy will be in far worse position in six months.'

'Confusing rubbish from the G7+EU is propaganda that leads to totalitarianism.'

'The total bullshit coming from the G7 is absolutely astounding,' Armstrong added. 'Boris Johnson had the nerve to assert that it was critical that the pandemic leave no "permanent scar" or inequality. This is nothing more than propaganda aimed at ushering in a new authoritarian society under the garb of 'equality' and 'fairness.'

The greatest concern of Western elites, he claims, is 'populism,' which essentially entails awakening the populace to the true goal of this pandemic and its associated 'Great Reset' and Agenda-2030. According to Armstrong, the ruling oligarchy is "as hopelessly corrupt as Julius Ceasar"... The G7 has pledged to higher spending to "assist" the developing countries deal with a crisis that they created. Of course, the G7 has promised money to combat climate change.'

People should understand that the G7-EU agenda 'leads to only one thing: totalitarianism,' or the technocratic-communist world dictatorship we have been warned about for so long, and in which our last liberties, as well as a large portion of our prosperity, will be permanently lost.

'Interesting picture of helpless leaders,' says Strategic Culture Foundation.

In an editorial, the Strategic Culture Foundation also humiliates the G7+EU. 'This forum has devolved into an anachronism that no longer reflects world reality.'

The SCF even witnesses a "disturbing event" in Cornwall. While presenting themselves as 'the world's saviors,' Western politicians come across as 'impotent and frivolous,' especially by further inflaming world differences by targeting Russia and China as so-called (false) 'democracies,' which are considered to be 'autocracies.' This is classic Alinksy jargon for 'accusing your opponent of what you are guilty of.'

'These affluent elite fosters phony conflicts between countries rather than genuine cooperation and peace.'

As a result, the SCF correctly notes that the G7+EU is nothing more than an instrument for consolidating US global hegemony. 'It's a pitiful performance... Biden is attempting to encourage his Western allies to be more antagonistic to China and Russia.' What does this have to do with the epidemic... or bettering the lives of billions of underprivileged people? 'Precisely: nothing.'

'Bitter irony: one of the agenda items is'sustainable development.' The G7 essentially reflects an unsustainable world order: a wealthy elite that fosters phony tensions between countries rather than actual cooperation and peace.' As a result, the G7+EU leaders, set on increasing power and control, are the most existential threat, rather than the answer.

It is therefore past time for anti-democratic autocrats like Biden, Johnson, Draghi, Merkel, and Macron, as well as all their lackeys in other Western capitals and globalist organizations like the WEF and the IMF, to permanently clear the field before they plunge our entire planet into even greater misery with, say, new pandemics.

Table of Contents

Chapter 1: Hyperinflation?

For years, we have been amazed that most people seem to believe it is normal for central banks to continue creating unimaginable amounts of money out of thin air at the push of a button so that governments can continue to spend massive amounts of money while believing that their purchasing power will be maintained.

Anyone who has taken two economics classes in high school knows that this is against all financial and fiscal laws, and it will result in a play sooner or later. It's almost here: the Bank of America announces HYPERinflation. This means that the currency's value will plummet, and the costs of most products and services would skyrocket.

According to annual estimates, the number of US corporations reporting (high) inflation has climbed by about 800%. As a result, Bank of America cannot help but notice this "At the very least, it suggests that 'temporary' hyperinflation is on the way.

Commodities (+28%), consumer prices (+36%), transportation (+35%), and manufactured products (+35%) are particularly vulnerable to price increases. Although the BoA believes it will remain'manageable,' hyperinflation is a process that intrinsically shows that something is spiraling out of control.

Exorbitant prices

This means that, among other things, citizens will eventually have to pay significantly more for almost everything at an escalating rate. Actually, we can observe this disguised high inflation in the increasing property prices (after all, these are not associated with a strong economic recovery, but with a government-funded debt economy). Furthermore, an increasing number of consumers are complaining that their weekly shopping have grown significantly more expensive in a relatively short period of time.

The end of prosperity is now in sight.

As depressing as it may be to read, the end of Western affluence is now in sight. Indeed, the situation in Europe is not dissimilar to that in the United States, and in some ways is far worse.

Consider the seemingly endless sovereign debts of Italy, Greece, and Spain, as well as France and Belgium. Furthermore, large European systemic banks like Deutsche Bank, Société Générale, and UniCredit are technically bankrupt.

The Green Deal and the Great Reset

On top of that, the EU's "Green Deal" and the World Economic Forum's "Excellent Reset. The former will make energy, transportation, and food virtually unaffordable for millions of people, while the latter will permanently erase the few vestiges of freedom and self-determination we have left, putting 35 to 41 percent of people out of work, according to WEF data.

While the West is tearing itself apart as a result of the realization of this climate dystopia, China and Russia have already begun to seize the baton from us.

Chapter 2: Debts are at an all-time high

The pandemic fraud has dragged the West further into debt than WW2 - Britain's largest pension fund (No. 6 in the world) tells investors that withdrawing money may take up to 95 days, and warns of probable insolvency.

The impending financial system collapse is the secret driver of the continuation of the corona pandemic fake measures and the frightening developments in Ukraine. Actually, this is the same problem that existed from 2008 to 2011, since it was only "fixed" with negative interest rates and massive sums of new digital money, which benefited mainly governments, shareholders, and large financial players. Now that the IMF has warned in a study that government debts have never been so high since WWII, this mega catastrophe, which will have far-reaching effects for ordinary people, might erupt at any time.

We've been writing about this for years, and now the IMF is warning that national debts have never been so high since World War II. The Corona crisis has been utilized as an excuse worldwide to practically create 'money like water,' because it is now worth nothing. The entire amount involved in Europe alone is a monstrous €130 billion, or almost one-third of the total national debt until 2019.

The New Great Depression has only been postponed.

If half of the economy had not been put on a drip since last year, we would currently be in a deeper Depression than the 1930s. So, what do you think is a good solution? Try to recall your first high school economics lesson, or the question that nearly every child has asked their parents at some point in their lives: "Why don't we just put money on the copy machine so that we always have enough and can buy copies?" "wealthy

We're assuming we don't have to answer these questions? If that's the case, you should stop reading and return to the mainstream propaganda media, which appears to have no idea what's going on (and if they did, they may not write about it until the crisis is a fait accompli and irreversible fact).

Is the crisis resolved? Greece's debt has already reached 200 percent of GDP.

The newest IMF 'Fiscal Monitor' report offers a bleak picture: government debts have never been proportionally so high since the end of WW2, the deadliest conflict ever fought. Do you recall the Greek crisis, which jeopardized the whole Eurozone and EU and was only just averted? Greece's federal debt has climbed to 160 percent of GDP. The country had to be'rescued' with several rescue packages totaling hundreds of billions of euros from countries such as the Germany.

Greece's national debt has now risen to more than 200 percent of GDP. What do you think, did this 'rescue' help?

At least not for the Greek people or the Greek economy. They simply received crumbs. The only ones "saved" were the European banks, who were "paid" by the European taxpayer for their debts to Greece in this especially deceptive manner. In the media, we were informed that we had 'rescued' the Greeks, but in reality, just like in 2008, we had saved the banks - the exact ones who had gotten us into this mess.

For example, the number of IC beds has been cut in half, resulting in Europe's lowest per capita level. Then, in 2020, a flu-like respiratory virus arose, the threat of which was purposely inflated in order to push through all sorts of punitive freedom-restricting restrictions. We do it for the sake of caring (after we have wrecked it first)'. No, 'we' do it to prepare the populace for a bank crisis-lockdown.

Banks must be bailed out again.

It is now 2021, and the banks must be saved once more. As we have previously stated, Europe's major systemic banks, such as Deutsche Bank and Société Générale, are technically bankrupt. At the same time, the pandemic myth has driven industrialized countries deeper into debt than World War II did, and the ECB has lately taken further moves that further erode our purchasing power and wealth.

Nobody is talking about the need to get out of debt anymore. All parties - governments and corporations - hope that interest rates will remain zero or negative in perpetuity, and that money will continue to play no role in the state. An increase in interest rates is, indeed, the worst-case situation. Even if it is minor, it will quickly force two much larger European debt nations, Italy and Spain, into state bankruptcy. Rescue is out of the question since it would cost trillions of euros. As a result, the collapse of any of these two countries automatically entails the collapse of the eurozone.

'Reorganization contributions,' but from whom?

As a result, the IMF suggests that nations begin levying 'clean-up payments' on incomes, assets, and earnings - a somewhat perplexing advice, considering that only robust and sustained economic development can potentially bring us back from the brink of this systemic disaster. If you then tax the already distressed business sector even more harshly, you will only have the opposite effect: the crisis will be exacerbated and intensified, hundreds of thousands of businesses will fail, and countless people will lose their jobs.

And there is nothing more to be gotten from the already strained people. Even higher taxes and even deeper cutbacks will drive significant swaths of the poor and middle classes into abject poverty. Governments have no choice but to turn to draconian financial repression, which will hurt the ordinary citizen, but notably the lowest-paid and most vulnerable. Millions of people will soon be unable to afford their housing/energy bills and foodstuffs on their own. Most of us will have to tighten our belts both metaphorically and practically.

Some analysts predict "Weimar"-style hyperinflation, which will utterly deplete our purchasing power. Given the current extremely perilous circumstances for many residents and businesses, even a considerably lower inflation rate of 3% to 4% will be the ultimate blow. Government bonds, life insurance, pension money, and savings will be worthless in no time.

The world's sixth insurer has issued a 'insolvency' warning.

Signs that the financial system crisis is approaching are also obvious in the United Kingdom, where Aviva, the country's largest insurer/pension fund and the world's sixth, has notified its clients that it might take up to 95 days before they may withdraw money from their accounts.

Even more frightening is the direct warning that " If a bank/insurer/pension fund employs that phrase at all, it is a signal of exceedingly significant, most probable insurmountable difficulties.

Gold, silver, and currency have been eliminated from the United Kingdom.

Without explanation, a large sum of gold, silver, and cash was unexpectedly withdrawn from the United Kingdom and transported to Qatar recently. The Bank of International Settlements (the BIS bank in Basel, the "central bank of central banks") documented a $1.8 billion payment from the Hillary Clinton Foundation to the Qatari Central Bank (QCB).

Possible causes vary from the UK's impending financial collapse to a conflict with Russia in which British towns may be annihilated with nuclear weapons.

Citizens and businesses will own NOTHING in the digital eurozone.

We've been warning for years that a systemic catastrophe is on the way, and it appears to be almost here. This catastrophe, which might be precipitated by a false flag cyber-attack (allegedly by Russia?), would be used to push through the 'Great Reset,' which is nothing more than the installation of an unprecedentedly harsh and exceedingly draconian technocratic communist climate-vaccine tyranny.

In financial and economic terms, this implies that the euro will be totally digital, that EVERYTHING will be state-owned (even your own body), and that citizens and businesses will be forever bereft of any kind of property or voice in the issue. The World Economic Forum also expects a permanent unemployment rate of 35 percent to 41 percent, as well as the implementation of a basic income that will be just enough to keep people alive.

Do you want the great reset?

This is what is coming, and it cannot be stopped. Even if the mass of the people woke up at the last minute and revolted against this, a 'Great Reset' would still be required, but of a completely different magnitude than that of the WEF and the globalists in Washington, Brussels, London, Paris, Berlin, Rome, and The Hague. Their reset concentrates all power and riches in the hands of a small elite club, whilst the Reset that we truly require achieves the reverse.

The technically insolvent Deutsche Bank has warned that the EU's 'Green Deal,' which is intended to enable the 'Great Reset,' will really trigger a mega-crisis and herald the entrance of an eco-dictatorship that would destroy our current affluence.

In any case, last years, the European people overwhelmingly voted for parties that want to adopt, and are currently implementing, the EU's Green Deal and the World Economic Forum's Reset initiative (at least, if the election results are correct). When their false promises and visions of a technocratic climate paradise turn out to have unleashed a veritable hell on earth for almost everyone, looking in the mirror and asking yourself in bewilderment "how did we ever let it get this far?" will be the only thing left for this gullible and apathetic people with their insufferable slave mentality.

We apologize for concluding this way, but as we observe more and more individuals wearing mouth caps even outside in the sun, there is just no reason to believe that sobriety and common sense will ever return to normal. I'm concerned that this inky dark spirit of purposefully cultivated and fanned societal fear of death and insanity will only go after a great deal of sorrow and sorrow.

Chapter 3: Money will be worthless

The impending financial mega-crisis will be exploited to complete the communist 'Great Reset.'

While the attention of both the government and the media remains almost totally on Corona, highly disturbing changes in the EU are going place in the background, which are likely to have far-reaching ramifications for our economic and buying power in the short to medium term. Because interest rates on government bonds have begun to climb again, the ECB will purchase more government debt in the coming months. Furthermore, the de facto technically bankrupt financial sector is in much more difficulties as a result of the fabricated monetary crisis. 'The only thing keeping the European Commission together any more is the ECB's magical money tree,' argues expert Alasdair Macleod. If you've ever attended two economics classes, you should know where such a thing is ""Money Tree" ALWAYS leads to: "This is a horror show in the making."

The EUSSR is a done deal, both politically and financially.

Critics sometimes refer to the European Union as the EUSSR, and by 2021, none of that is an exaggeration - rather the reverse. Politically, the EU has long functioned in the same way as the former Soviet Union: the Politburo, an unelected club of bureaucrats known as the European Commission, determines policy and sends its 'wishes' (=orders) to the European Council of Heads of Government, who debate them for show and then send these orders to their own - in name only - independent countries, where the parliaments are elected.

To maintain the pretense of a European democracy, the EU maintains its own "parliament," in which all members are paid exorbitant salaries, bonuses, and pensions for participating in this grand spectacle while maintaining mute about the fact that they have nothing, absolutely nothing to contribute. The only time this parliament appeared to have any 'power' was when it sent a European Commission home, but it was most likely staged, especially in retrospect, because it was at that time that the European people began to wake up to the EU 'socialist' (in the Marxist sense) character and purpose.

Recently, the ECB discreetly took the next step toward the euro's, the euro/Target-2 system's, and its own demise. Contrary to previous pronouncements, the bank has chosen to acquire more government bonds in the coming months as interest rates rise globally. If this tendency continues, the entire eurozone network will go bankrupt. 'And that network is a mouthful of rotting apples,' Macleod adds. 'It is the outcome of not only a broken system, but also of measures designed to keep Spain's interest rates from rising in 2012.'

'Whatever it takes,' the euro is 'saved' at the expense of citizens.

At the time, ECB President Mario Draghi famously stated that he would rescue the euro "whatever it takes." What he didn't tell us was that the cost of this "whatever it takes" will be borne by European savers and pension funds. Because of the growing debt, Christine Lagarde's action must be considerably bigger than that of her predecessor, Mario Draghi. Ultimately, all Europeans will have to pay a high price for this, in the form of a significant and irreversible loss of buying power and wealth. The EU member states' glitzy years of prosperity are coming to an end.

Lagarde kicks Draghi's 'whatever it takes' mantra up a notch. The ECB, which professes to be "independent" but is fundamentally a political organization, has always served one purpose: to ensure that the unrestrained spending of the southern member states, in particular, is always covered.

For this goal, an inventive mechanism was devised: Italy and Spain alone owe the ECB system about €1 trillion. Germany, Luxembourg, Finland, and the Netherlands, on the other hand, are owed around € 1.6 trillion under this system, with Germany owing the lion's share (more than € 1 trillion). (In reality, tiny Luxembourg may be viewed as a bank masquerading as an independent state, one of the numerous gimmicks employed by the

ECB to make the EU's financial condition appear more favorable.)

Large mega-banks are technically bankrupt.

By purchasing government bonds, the ECB has already amassed a debt of € 345 billion, owing in part to the clandestine funding of France's rising government deficit. France is now one of the PIIGS countries, although this will never be formally acknowledged because France is seen as a'systemically important' state. Meanwhile, France's liabilities are beginning to weigh hard on the euro system, not least since the French mega-bank Société Générale, as well as Deutsche Bank and Italy's Unicredit, are technically functionally insolvent.

What the figures do not reveal is that the Bundesbank has already purchased billions of euros of German government debt on behalf of the ECB. The ever-increasing imbalance in the Target-2 system has arisen as a result of Italy, Spain, Greece, and Portugal, in particular, being saddled with an increasing number of 'bad' loans, or loans that can and will never be repaid. As a result, the 'zombie' financial systems in these nations had to be permanently fed by the ECB.

Bad loans and bad assets

The bad loans and other 'bad assets' were transferred to the euro system (and therefore, in particular, to

Germany, Finland, the Netherlands, and Luxembourg) during the 'bailout' of Greece, and subsequently to the Target-2 system during the 'bailout' of the Italian banks, which was disguised from the public. What is not included in the numbers is an even larger sum of €8.31 trillion (possibly more than €10 trillion) in short-term funding, which is basically non-existent in the eurozone.

In summary, if you have an average yearly salary of € 36,000, you can acquire a € 1 million loan from a bank without batting an eye, and the bank manager then says to you: "See what you can pay back, and when..." What do you think? Will this bank be able to survive for a long time? And can a central bank that then keeps these banks afloat for years be able to maintain its health for a long time?

'Like a group of drunks attempting to raise themselves staggeringly out of the gutter, European bank stock values have climbed alongside the markets. 'However, their ratings continue to be appallingly low,' says Macleod. The situation has deteriorated to the point that if one large eurozone bank fails, the entire system would fall like a house of cards.

The EU is a collapsing state, and its purchasing power will be wiped out.

The EU is showing all of the hallmarks of a crumbling state "the analyst continues This was most clear in the EU's reaction to Brexit, which can only be defined as stupid and infantile vengeance, regardless of the unpleasant implications for the bloc itself. Furthermore, the EU is unlikely to escape from lockdowns this year, which means that all member countries will be forced to continue incurring massive new debt in order to keep their economies afloat. The effects of highly harmful policies will be far worse for Europe than for the United States and China.

Large swaths of the economy, particularly SMEs, are on the point of collapse. When the trends in the commodities markets (oil, metals, food, etc.) are combined with the massive growth in the money supply, the result will be a worldwide loss of buying power. Because of its own structure, policies, and actions, the EU is entirely trailing behind China's economic rebound, which is now in full gear.

'And, because the ECB is in charge of everything's finance, the EU's problem will undoubtedly begin there. It will undoubtedly bring down the majority of the financial sector... It won't take a significant increase in interest rates to wipe it away.' The genuine worth of the 'value' and 'assets' claimed by the large Eurozone banks on their balance sheets is then revealed: 'basically NOTHING.' It's no surprise that capital flight from the Eurozone has increased. Money usually exits nations with terrible and wasteful policies, and it will soon be worthless.

'The system is purposely inflated in order to accomplish the communist Great Reset.'

If you're wondering, why aren't they doing something to avoid this? Then we'll respond: because, in our opinion, the system is being deliberately blown apart. A digital euro is already in the works, and it will eventually replace all currency. This new digital money system will most likely be launched during or shortly after the approaching financial mega-crisis, and will be gradually connected to everything (ID/passport, debit card, Covid card, and so on). All debts will be forfeited, and all 'assets,' all property, all funds, of all corporations and people, will be transferred to the state.

The 'Great Reset,' or the change of the once-successful E.E.C. free trade bloc into a European Soviet Union with a technocratic and profoundly communist regime, will then be completed. Then our prosperity, as well as all of our liberties and belongings, will be restored. (And you, as an entrepreneur, were overjoyed when the government pledged to reimburse you for 100 percent of your fixed expenditures! Do you honestly not know you've all walked right into a trap? That you will soon have nothing more to say regarding your own business and survival in this controlled economy?)

Look through the history books to gain a sense of how 'nice' life will be for us then. However, for the vast majority of people, such an appeal will fall on deaf ears. They voted even more heavily for allegedly 'liberal' parties that have for years adopted virtually entirely neo-Marxist EU policies.

To our great dismay, there appears to be just one thing left to do to bring the people back to their senses, and that is to experience a lot of suffering (again). With the hope that our surviving (grand)children will have learnt from these harsh lessons and will be able and willing to construct a far healthier society, a world where Big Banks, Big Pharma, Big Tech, Big Military, and Big Government, in other words: Big Corruption, have no place.

Chapter 4: History repeats itself?

The parallel between Germany 1914-1923 and the West 2010-2021 is seamless.

Is history repeating itself in every way, but on an even larger scale? It looks suspiciously like it. Just as in the 1910s - 1920s, unimaginable amounts of money created out of thin air have been used to buy up massive amounts of debt and create enormous wealth, and everyone wants a piece of the pie. Wall Street chief Michael Burry, nicknamed 'Big Short' because he was the first investor to foresee the subprime crisis (2007-2010), warns that hyperinflation will suddenly break out, just as it did in the Weimar Republic.

'People have said I didn't warn last time,' hedge fund manager 'Big Short' Burry responded to the storm of reactions to his hyperinflation prediction. *'I did, but nobody listened. So I'm warning now. And again, no one listens. But I will have proof that I warned.'*

Recently, Burry tweeted that the US government's MMT (Modern Monetary Theory, the de facto communist course that has been followed in the EU for some 7 years) 'invites inflation'. The Biden administration is spending trillions to keep the economy and society 'afloat' in the midst of the corona crisis, but will achieve the opposite as soon as they are gradually opened again. When demand rises again, all that money will explode the prices and costs of workers, which will be

the beginning of inflation, or hyperinflation, spiraling
out of control.

'It couldn't go on'

Bank of America CIO Michael Hartnett also compares
the 'tsunami of fiscal stimulus' and monetization of the
huge debt burden (which has been done in the EU since
2014 with massive buybacks of sovereign debt and with
negative interest rates, at the expense of savings,
pensions and purchasing power) directly to the
situation in Germany (the Weimar Republic) after World
War I.

Jens Parsson wrote in 1974 that the period 1914 - 1923
was characterized by "great prosperity, at least for
those profiting from the 'boom.' There was a 'can't wait'
atmosphere. Prices were stable, and the stock market
and business were doing fine. The German Mark even
initially became worth more than the dollar, and for a
while was the strongest currency in the world.

Yet there were "simultaneous groups with poverty.
More and more people fell out of the easy money, and
could not get into it. Crime rose sharply.' The common
man 'became demoralized', because hard work and
saving yielded less and less, while others grew their
money from their lazy lounger, and became puissant
rich.

Everyone wanted a piece of the pie

Almost any form of enterprise, no matter how speculative, made money. The number of collapses and bankruptcies fell. The 'natural (economic) selection', whereby weak, badly run and/or non-essential companies fall and the stronger ones stay afloat, disappeared.

Speculation became one of the most important activities in Germany. Everyone wanted a piece of the pie, including citizens of almost all classes. Even elevator operators took part in investing. It was not production, innovation and achievement that created prosperity, but money and speculation. The Berlin stock exchange literally could not keep up with the volumes of securities traded.

1921/22 = 2021/22

And then came the blow, as sudden as it was devastating. All the marks that existed in the world in 1922 were not enough in November 1923 to buy a single newspaper or a ticket for the streetcar. 'That was the spectacular part of the collapse, but most of the real loss in (monetary) wealth had occurred much earlier. During these years, the structure quietly built itself up for this blow. The German inflation cycle lasted not one, but 9 years: 8 years of growth, and only 1 year of collapse.

You must have had your eyes closed very tightly for the past 10+ years to deny that Burry is doubly right when he writes that this 47-year-old analysis applies seamlessly to the 2010 - 2021 period, in which dollars (and euros) 'could just as easily have fallen from the sky... management teams got creative and took even more risks... and paid out debt-financed dividends to investors, or invested in risky growth opportunities.'

Citizens were massively invited and urged to invest their own money, just as they were then, because stock prices would only continue to rise anyway, as would house prices. In recent years, the highly speculative crypto market turned out to be the most profitable; some people who got in early became very rich, and were able to retire early.

And again we are on the brink of an unprecedented crash

As in 1921-1922, most people do not realize that exactly a century later, thanks to even worse speculative fever and unprecedentedly insane fiscal and monetary policies, we are once again on the verge of such a sudden huge crash, Burry also warns. The 'Weimar' hyperinflation wiped out all prosperity in no time, except that of the 'elite' and a few major financial players. Bitter poverty and misery awaited the people, which became the fertile ground for the rise of the Nazis.

And there are more chilling parallels. Just as in the 1930s, in our time there has been mass fear-mongering, people have been pitted against each other, and harsh dictatorial measures have been taken that have ended our freedoms and many of our rights. Just as in the 1940s, medical experiments are being conducted on people, but now not just in closed camps, but worldwide, with controversial vaccinations, on billions at a time. And just like in the 1920s, most people didn't want to hear about a crisis; after all, the trees were growing to the sky, and they would always continue to do so.

However, politicians have long been aware that the biggest financial crisis of all time is imminent. In order to nip mass panic and protests in the bud, a common respiratory virus was chosen as the pretext to destroy the freedoms and rights of citizens step by step. We wrote from the beginning that the curfew has nothing to do with public health and safety, but everything to do with capitalizing on this impending crisis. And what do you think? Meanwhile, there is speculation in The Hague about possibly extending the curfew to noon, "should that be necessary.

Is there escape from this 'Great Reset'?

Count on it that it WILL be necessary, however not for a viral mutation, as will again be falsely claimed, but to keep the people locked up in their carefully crafted emergency measures and laws, so that they cannot

33

revolt en masse when it turns out that almost everything they took for granted to hold 'value' forever - including their purchasing power, homes, jobs, investments and pensions - is gone for good, and this will have been done on purpose too, because it carries out a political-ideological agenda: the 'Great Reset'.

Is there an escape, an alternative? Yes, but only if we peacefully resist by refusing en masse to continue to contribute to our own demise.

Chapter 5: Incoming food crisis?

Europe has entered a comprehensive systemic crisis, with Germany already blaming 'cyber assaults' (of course, by 'the Russians,' which should prepare the populace for a massive conflict – 'The loss of 0.025 percent of the world's population does not warrant the ruin of the global economy.'

The 'Great Reset' of our secure and affluent society, purposefully started in motion by an airway virus, is going to be felt much more strongly. More and more signs point to Europe being on the verge of a food catastrophe with sky-high prices. Meanwhile, politicians and the media continue to pass on, rationalize, and sometimes even praise all of the blame for the suffering that has already occurred and is on its way.

The Food Price Index (FFPI) of the United Nations Food and Agriculture Organization (FAO) increased by 2.3 points (2.2 percent) in one month to 107.5 in December 2020, marking the seventh consecutive increase. The FFPI stood at 53.1 points in 2002, peaked at 131.9 points in 2011 as a result of the financial crisis, and then fell to slightly under 100.

Food, energy, and banking crises all at once

That governments exploit completely normal, natural, and harmless to the great majority of people biological alterations to prolong and/or enhance lockdown measures and limits on liberty, food supply lines will experience similar challenges as the electronics sector is presently experiencing (major shortage of microchips).

There are already fears in Germany that fruit and vegetable shortages are impending. They have also found a so-called cause: cyber attacks, which will, of course, be blamed on "the Russians." The horrible World Economic Forum of Klaus Schwab, the diabolical brain behind the 'Great Reset,' also anticipates cyber attacks on the power system and the financial sector.

Historical concept: blaming others for your own actions.

Basic food and energy are also getting increasingly pricey, and serious issues with bank accounts and internet payments should have you ready to commit to a massive conflict, most likely against Russia. In reality, energy disruptions will be created by a shift away from coal, oil, and gas, since a shift to unreliable and expensive wind, solar, and biomass is necessary. Furthermore, the next major banking crisis has been in the works for years, and it will be exploited to push through a fully digital payment system with a digital euro.

It's an old, known historical principle that's been utilized a lot: blame the party you consider the adversary for the issues you've created, and you'll have their support. Unfortunately, few people read history books now, or they refuse to learn from them ('this time we'll do it better,' 'this time things will be different') because they believe they are far brighter. (What is our opinion? Quite the contrary).

Or you have studied for it, and you have used the societal manipulating and undermining neo-Marxist strategies that authoritarian and dictatorial governments have used so many times before to your own people in an exceedingly sophisticated way, and let them be thankful for it as well.

'Did they have inside information, or is this a shady scheme?'

In this regard, American economist Martin Armstrong points to the well-known 'Event 201' pandemic simulation in October 2019, in which everything done from 2020 onwards was discussed, drafted, and worked out in detail in advance, complete with the deliberate sowing of fear and panic over a common coronavirus.

'Did they have foresight into the future, or is there a nefarious plot to lower population and CO_2, neatly creating global slaughter, as some now believe? Such conspiracy ideas often emerge when there are secret meetings and elite groups that believe they are exalted above the lower classes, which they see as the 'Great Scum.'

Conspiracy theories, on the other hand, are long gone, because all of these wicked schemes can be read, heard, and seen openly in the publications of major groups like the WEF. Although some of them, such as "In 2030 you will own nothing and be happy," were taken off after causing quite a sensation. That won't stop authoritarian bureaucrats from forcing this dreadful future on you and me (but not on themselves) in 2030. (but probably much earlier).

Food scarcity has caused widespread societal unrest (and possibly war)

In any event, food shortages and increasing costs are certain between now and 2024. 'This will cause significant social and political instability,' warns Armstrong. 'The EU government's mishandling might be their undoing. After all, as a result of such mismanagement, many people have lost their employment as a result of having to stay at home during the crisis, and their purchasing power has plummeted at the same time. This is the worst-case scenario, and it makes me wonder if these leaders are indeed that foolish, or simply that cunning.'

We believe both of them. Devious, because this systemic crisis has been planned to all intents and purposes, including fully controlling and directing the mainstream media, with the goal of creating a dictatorial EU superstate that will be (and already is) a technocratic mix of the former Soviet system and today's communist China.

Stupid, because they believe that their 'Great Reset / Build Back Better / Green New Deal' coup against free society will work in the long run, so that by 2030, the Bidens of our time will have fulfilled their hoped-for climatic utopia. Evidently, these individuals have lost their sense of reality, since otherwise, they should realize that with an all-or-nothing approach, nothing of our civilization would survive by 2030 at the latest.

In any event, Armstrong believes that the world is unprepared for a food crisis, which will surely be triggered by the continuation of the current measures. Shortages will be more severe in major cities. The high VAT and taxes in Europe will be the final nail in the coffin for many. Then supermarkets do not need to be supplied for only a few days for widespread panic, anarchy, and violence to erupt.

According to the economist, stock market speculators will be punished, but we believe a political offender, most likely Russian President Vladimir Putin, will also be implicated. If that is the case, it is convenient if you have already sparked a large regional conflict in, say, Ukraine, and maybe the Middle East, before then. After all, we've seen how easily supply networks can be disrupted by a single container ship (Suez Canal).

Bill Gates is one of the most significant contributors to this catastrophe.

Armstrong then offers another 'conspiracy theory,' according to which Bill Gates is now the largest owner of farmland in the United States. True or not, it has been proved that he has 'purchased' the WHO and has it in his pocket, as well as the American CDC and, probably, all equivalent agencies in Europe. Furthermore, he has stock in every major pharmaceutical business and is the main force behind the GAVI vaccination partnership. So, though Gates will undoubtedly be one of the most significant contributors to the years-long catastrophe, the Western media, which he co-controls, will never be permitted to publish that.

Hundreds of thousands of farms have vanished in both America and Europe over the last decade, mostly due to ever-increasing taxes and ever-stricter 'environment' rules and legislation. Governments were able to acquire enormous tracts of land at extremely low costs for projects like as housing, "sustainable" energy, and "nature restoration." This long-standing anti-farming strategy threatens to amplify the looming food catastrophe.

The loss of 0.025 percent of the world's population does not warrant the ruin of the global economy.

'Meanwhile, there is a rush to immunize everyone against a disease that is no more fatal than the flu,' Armstrong added. 'The number of Covid fatalities is so overblown that our politicians are either the stupidest or the most deceitful persons on the planet. During the Spanish flu, 50 million people died, accounting for 3.125 percent of the world's population at the time (1.6 billion). There are now 7.8 billion people on the planet, and 2 million deceased individuals account for only 0.02564 percent of that. This in no way excuses the collapse of the global economy.'

The Nuremberg Agreements have been ignored and even reversed.

'The mainstream media shamelessly applauds the lockdowns and terrorizes the population.' It is becoming clear that immunizations protect no one from catching Covid and may even put them in greater danger if the population is wiped out by one of the new mutations. Meanwhile, pharmaceutical firms are completely insulated from responsibility. All international leaders agreed at Nuremberg to prohibit such medical experiments on the general people if they had not yet (or not properly) been tested on animals. The vaccinations that are being administered have not even been tested on rats or mice.'

(This is due, in part, to far-left, Marxist 'woke' thinking, which has stripped people of any higher spirituality and regards them as nothing more than a biological machine incapable of transcending animal life. Indeed, by utilizing humans as guinea pigs rather than animals, people are positioned under animals. It goes without saying that this heinous anti-human mindset paves the way for a bloodbath, a genocide, the likes of which the world has never seen before and will most likely never see again (since there will be far too few of us remaining).

Chapter 6: Another world war?

The Russian reaction to the provocations of US bombers was unprecedented: three nuclear submarines burst through the polar ice at the same time. The United States could be annihilated in minutes from that vantage point.

The tremendously concerning situation in Ukraine is now reaching the (alternative) media. Analyst Tom Luongo now claims that the West, led by Joe Biden, is preparing for a confrontation with Russia in Ukraine, maybe as soon as after the Orthodox Passover (May 2). The fundamental reason is because the Kremlin refuses to sign on to the World Economic Forum's, United Nations', and European Union's Great Reset 2030 climate plan. Western politicians have gone wild to the point that they are making the fatal mistake of assuming that President Putin will not dare to defend his nation to the death against this worldwide coup. In doing so, Washington, Brussels, and The Hague are deliberately putting themselves at danger of a large-scale nuclear battle erupting.

Now, the long-desired conflict against Russia threatens to put a stop to the European fantasy of a "climate paradise" in 2030, which would, in any event, finish years early in a dreadful nightmare full of communist poverty and technocratic oppression for 99 percent of the people.

Who is the true "soulless killer"?

Biden had only been president for a few months when he referred to Putin as a "killer without a soul." The Russian president answered with "it takes one to know one," in his usual calm and masterful manner, and then invited Biden to a direct discussion.

Of course, Biden declined, because the demented Biden, who frequently forgets where he is and who he is speaking to during speeches (there is now footage showing him with cards in his hand with "who is who" pictures on them, as well as a complete script that he has to follow), is clearly no match for the Russian leader. The Democrats are well aware of this, which is why they want to keep him away from the press as much as possible.

'And then there was that humiliating press conference the other day.' Is he running for re-election in 2024? He won't even be alive at that point. But, hey, he didn't run in 2020 either, so what's the difference?" scoffs Luongo.

Russian retaliation to American provocations

In any event, relations between the two superpowers have been 'appalling' since the nomination of phony President Biden in a flashy political coup. Americans are doing nothing to change this, in fact, exactly the contrary. Recently, Biden dispatched strategic B-52 bombers to launch a fake strike on Russia across the

North Pole. The jets returned to Canada, but a response from the Kremlin was unavoidable. Three Russian nuclear submarines (a one-time occurrence) broke through the polar ice at the same time. From that vantage point, the United States could be completely annihilated in fifteen minutes.

Obama says Ukraine is 'Biden's project.'

Ukraine is 'Biden's project,' declared Barack Obama. The Bidens are embroiled in corruption in Ukraine, as we have widely exposed in recent years.

According to Luongo, the situation in Ukraine is "far more hazardous" than we are told. We've previously given you one possible explanation, and it's not very reassuring: the Western elite may try to overwhelm the populace with a sudden conflict, falsely presenting it as a "Russian surprise strike," to which "of course, we must reply promptly." You may not be allowed time to examine what is actually going on, which is that this conflict is only supporting the interests of the 'Great Reset' climate elite, who must be pushed through at the expense of the general public.

The escalating war in Ukraine is "all of this and more." The initiative to admit Ukraine to NATO and the EU has long been a goal of neocons such as Victoria Nuland and neoliberals such as Joe Biden. It is a key component of the World Economic Forum's ambition to encircle

Russia, obstructing the goal of Eurasian integration that may serve as a bulwark against their 'brave new world.'

The West wishes to compel Russia and China to conform to the Great Reset.

Biden has invited Putin and Chinese President Xi Jinping to a climate meeting in April, the agenda of which will be dictated by the World Economic Forum. Because both Putin and Xi have stated that they would not engage in the Great Reset and Agenda 2030, as well as Klaus Schwab's "Fourth Industrial Revolution" (in actuality, the Great Industrial Deconstruction), this meeting is bound to fail from the start (though no doubt some lip service will be paid, but after that Russia and China will just go their separate ways).

'This summit appears to be a massive waste of time, because everyone across the globe will be threatened with what they can anticipate from the West in terms of policy - until someone finally puts these lunatic individuals out of their misery,' Luongo said. 'For example, the United Kingdom under dictator Boris Johnson is falling more and further into a full totalitarian nightmare as a result of Covid-19, while anti-Russian propaganda is reaching record heights.'

War in the Donbass, potentially as soon as tomorrow

Ukraine is "directly implicated in all of this crap about climate change." Putin also believes that Biden will not allow any escalation in Ukraine because he is tethered to it and must complete the work he began in 2014 with the toppling of (the democratically elected president) Viktor Yanukovich. As a result, we will witness something far worse than Victoria Nuland's "cookie campaign" for liberty. We shall have a fight over the Donbass shortly, most likely shortly after Orthodox Easter and the melting of the winter.'

According to Luongo, Putin has made tremendous efforts to halt this fatal downward cycle, 'because he understands where this leads.' It will be a showdown in which Putin will have to either watch Ukraine launch a war against the Russian-speaking people in the Donbass and Crimea with Western support, or interfere anyhow, knowing that the West would instantly use this to paint him as the 'aggressor.'

The West is preparing for an escalation; the EU has refused dialogue for years.

The West, according to Luongo, has no choice but to escalate since it stands to gain nothing from a return to quiet, peace, and collaboration. 'Russia must be subdued or destroyed for the Great Reset to work and Europe to remain an important global actor.' That entails control of the Black Sea and the conquest of Crimea.'

Russian Foreign Minister Sergei Lavrov recently voiced worry that the EU has not maintained diplomatic connections with the Kremlin after the 2014 vote, in which the people of Crimea declared nearly overwhelmingly that they wanted to belong to the Russian homeland. 'Diplomacy between big nations has all but vanished.' Biden's plain reluctance to engage in open dialogue with Putin is a major concern.'

The Great Reset is hampered by Eurasian dominance over oil and gas.

Everything since the 'corona' of totalitarian and oppressive measures in the West, including the gradual destruction of SMEs and freedom, is in line with the WEF's 'Great Reset,' which includes the total destruction of the 'fossil' economy and, with it, the end of energy security and affordability for Western citizens.

However, if the production of oil, gas, and coal continues under Eurasian control, the Atlanteans' megalomaniacal ambitions will never come true. There isn't much time left for them to impose their worldwide communist climate-vaccine tyranny, since Western public opposition to the entire devastation of their society and future grows by the day.

The West will not have a joyful finish to the war.

'If there is a conflict in the Donbass this spring, it will not have a nice conclusion in which America (and Europe) will continue in power in the future, but it will be the moment when we understand that our descent into irrelevance has hastened.'

With a bit of bad luck, this deterioration may even result in a nuclear battle, in which Russia (perhaps aided by China) decides to chop off the 'head of the serpent' that has been an ever-increasing threat to humanity's existence for so long. This may include a (limited) nuclear strike on cities like Washington, New York, London, Brussels, and Rome (the Vatican), as well as Los Angeles (Hollywood), Paris, Strasbourg, Berlin, Frankfurt, and The Hague.

We can be certain of one thing: if it were up to Vladimir Putin, it would never have come to that. It remains to be seen if there will be enough time for the fear, hunger for power, and sheer lunacy that have utterly overtaken the cities named to give way to a restoration of reason, sobriety, and, most importantly, true concern for the well and future of all residents. Unfortunately, the omens for this are now pointing in the other direction.

If China joins in, WW3 is a fact!

If China becomes embroiled in a major battle with the West, such as a war with Taiwan, Japan and Australia might be targeted, and hostilities might erupt between North and South Korea, India and Pakistan, India and China, Iran and Saudi Arabia, and Iran and Israel. Then World War III will become a reality.

For the time being, we are anticipating that the final major global conflagration will not occur until somewhere between 2025 and 2030. Nonetheless, everyone will see that a conflict in Ukraine might easily tumble all the other dominoes far sooner.

Chapter 7: Global currency?

Banker: 'The whole financial system will be destroyed if you do this'

There has been a lot of talk lately about the Reddit 'crowd', ordinary people who are collectively trying to bring down the big financial players (banks, hedge funds) by first getting into GameStop (GME) en masse, and who have now turned to silver, whose price rose in no time to above $30, the highest level in 7 years. Megabank Goldman Sachs - quite often compared to a vampire squid - even warned its clients yesterday that if this "short squeeze" continues, the entire market could collapse. That will crash the entire global financial system. Isn't that exactly what the globalists and governments are waiting for? It will give them a perfect excuse for their planned "Great Reset" and the introduction of a digital world currency under a one-world authority.

In a short squeeze, the price of an asset such as a precious metal is pushed up so quickly and so high, that traders who had bet on the price falling are forced to buy, because otherwise their losses would be too high and they could go bankrupt. This drives the price up even further, which only fuels the "short squeeze.

With GameStop, investors lost about 6 billion, but with silver, the loss could be in the trillions in the extreme. All the banks combined cannot possibly cover that, and would go bankrupt. The entire financial system would collapse worldwide, causing unimaginable chaos and panic, and untold casualties.

'F*** the Banks'

One of the WallStreetBets users announced this 'attack' as follows:

'The Silver Bullion market is one of the most manipulated on earth. Any short squeeze in silver bullion shorts would be EPIC. We know that the billion dollar banks manipulate gold and silver to cover real inflation.

For both the industrial and monetary state, printing debt for the #1 inflation safeguard, silver, has never been more beneficial. Inflation corrected silver should be at $1000 instead of $25. Why don't we squeeze the $SLV to the real physical price.

Think of what this could bring. If profit doesn't interest you, think of the banks like JP Morgan that will be destroyed with it. Pinch the market... Buy $SLV and go all in... Demand physical delivery (of silver), if you can. F*** the banks.'

'I'm burning everything down, purely for revenge'

Another wrote that he is participating for purely personal reasons:

'I remember how the housing market crash sent a torpedo through my family. My father's concrete company collapsed almost overnight. My father lost his house. So did my uncle. I remember how my brother helped my father count some change on the kitchen table. That was all the money he had left.

While this was happening at my house, I watched hedge fund managers literally drink champagne while looking down on the Occupy Wall Street protesters. I will never forget that.

My father never recovered from that blow. He sank deeper and deeper into alcoholism, and is only a shadow of who he was, waiting to die.

This is all the money I have. I'd rather lose all that than give them what they need to destroy me. Taking money from me doesn't affect me, because I don't value it at all. I burn it all down purely to take revenge on them. This is for you, Dad.'

Banker: 'The whole financial system will be destroyed if you do this'

A banker, allegedly from JP Morgan Chase, warned on one of the 'Chan' forums that the Reddit people have no idea what they are doing:

'I work for a bank whose name I will not disclose. You idiots, you have no idea what you are doing. No idea how serious this is.

This is not a simple "get rich quick" game. If there is a short squeeze in silver, all banks will fail. Every bank. Eight of them are short on silver, and would have to pay trillions to cover their shorts if silver goes to four figures. The entire financial system will be destroyed if you do this.

Silver is to the banks what GME was to Melvin Capital. Is this what you guys want to happen in the middle of a pandemic? If the banks blow up, you will wipe out everyone who owns dollars. What the hell is wrong with you. America will be destroyed.

If you do this, don't think we won't take away your silver, just like we disabled your manipulated short squeeze stocks (GME). You un-American traitors have been warned.'

'Average citizen has had it with this system'

But 'the average citizen has had it all with the system,' American conservative radio host Hal Turner comments. 'This system was set up for the rich to protect the rich, by targeting the common man. Now the little guys have joined forces, stabbing the rich right in the heart.'

'One of them wrote: 'I'm burning it all down, purely to take revenge on them. If THIS is the intention of people fighting a financial war, things will quickly get out of hand. Therefore, make sure you have extra food and cash. This will continue for another week before SHTF ("all hell breaks loose"). That will happen if this continues. The suits are scared, guys. And rightly so.'

'We will give them their Great Reset'

But isn't a financial mega-crisis exactly what the globalists are after, so that they can then create 'ordo ab chao', order out of chaos: a New World Order under central governance, with a new digital world currency? Someone on the social network Gab.com is indeed announcing a 'Great Reset', but a different one than what the UN, WHO, WEF and EU are pushing for:

'The world elites want the Great Reset, to take away our money and introduce a universal basic income. We will give them the Great Reset, and collapse their Ponzi scheme (pyramid scheme), the Federal Reserve and the banks.

When everything is in ashes, we will reintroduce our local gold-based currency, or something else that cannot be multiplied infinitely. Time to return to sound money and sound trade. Universal Basic Work. You won't eat if you don't work.

A message to the bankers: you better buy gold and silver, because those dollars will be used to light the fire in the winter when this is all over.

You guys shouldn't have stolen the election. You shouldn't have manipulated the financial system. You shouldn't have ignored the Constitution, and most importantly, you shouldn't have turned against the Holy Bible.

Action as Jesus, or just on behalf of "the devil"?

Is what the Reddit group is doing, then, perhaps a modern version of a well-known action of Jesus Christ, who went into the Temple and turned over the tables of the money changers and merchants, and drove them out of the Temple with a whip, saying that "you have made this place of worship a den of robbers"? (Mark 11:15-18)

Or are they just giving the globalist bankers, politicians and multi-millionaires a great excuse to shift the blame for the planned financial mega-crash onto the common man, and using this as an opportunity to realize their long-dreamed one-world currency under one-world government with a diabolical 'Great Reset'?

Chapter 8: Fuel problems?

Is this a practice run for the upcoming big cyber strike on the West?

According to experts, the cyber attack on the main fuel pipeline in the United States could have been resolved in a matter of hours, and thus bears all the hallmarks of a 'false flag' operation designed to bring the American people completely to their knees before the emerging communist UN/WEF climate-vaccine dictatorship. The first gas stations have run out of fuel, and those that still have it are hiking their prices dramatically. Fuel may be rationed for an extended period of time, and once this occurs, food will unavoidably follow.

According to one IT expert, the Colonial Pipeline from Houston (Texas) to Linden (New Jersey) could have been operational again in a matter of hours since damaged gear could have been swiftly replaced since most computer servers nowadays are Virtual Machines (VMs). If just the software had been damaged, the outage would have just been a few minutes long. As a result, the pipeline had many backups in every way.

Because no recovery was announced until the end of the week, this IT specialist believes that the gasoline shortages are being caused arbitrarily. Diesel is still used in trucks, but only for a limited time. When they come to a halt today or tomorrow, the stores will swiftly empty, threatening absolute fear and pandemonium.

After a week, the country will come to a halt, after two weeks, the drinking water supply will be jeopardized, and after four weeks, civilization will be finished.

North Carolina's governor has proclaimed a state of emergency and has temporarily (?) rationed petrol. The pumps of major businesses such as Shell and BP are now facing supply issues as well.

Is this a dress rehearsal for the recently anticipated major cyber-attack?

Unless the government repairs the pipeline within a few days, the already-started run on the final traces of gasoline will be followed by a run on the supermarkets. Indeed, it is highly conceivable that this 'false flag' was a practice run for the massive cyber-crisis previously foreshadowed by the WEF, which is to crush the whole West - including Europe - in order to crush the final remains of opposition to communist control of our country.

Of course, the Russians will be blamed for everything, which, as our readers well aware, is designed to rally the still-crazy masses behind the also-planned Third World War against Russia (and possibly China).

Complaining? Not if you voted in favor of this system.

Voters of the leftist and socialist parties, in particular, should not complain, because these parties, like almost all left-wing opposition parties, openly support the Great Reset / Build Back Better / Agenda-21/2030 agenda and have been doing everything in their power for many years to make this future a reality for you and your (grand)children.

Except for themselves, of course, because, like in every communist and fascist dictatorships throughout history, the power elite will make certain that they are never impacted by their own rock-hard freedom and wealth-destroying laws.

Chapter 9: Climate propaganda

'Climate activists will kill the economy,' says top economist Armstrong. - Donald Trump: 'Alarmists always want the same thing: ultimate power to rule, modify, and control every area of our life - Let's be hopeful!'

Greta Thunberg, shamelessly abused by the green-left liberal elite, said at the Globe Economic Forum in Davos that our world is "still on fire," and so demands not a reduction in CO2 emissions, but a full halt to the use of all fossil fuels. Granting even half of her irrational request will result in the utter downfall of our contemporary civilization, claiming hundreds of millions of lives and plunging billions into deep poverty and suffering, partly because the temperature is really growing colder due to a new solar minimum that began this year.

'Climate activists will wreck the economy,' says one expert.

Martin Armstrong, America's top economist, sees things dimly. He is in contact with folks in Davos who are providing him with behind-the-scenes information. 'I have repeatedly stated that there is NOTHING we can do to avoid what is about to occur. Only when the economy begins to crumble and burn down will world leaders take action. Climate activists will make certain that the economy is destroyed. They are socialists who wish to penalize those who drive and heat their houses.'

With photographs of Newfoundland's big blizzard, he says sarcastically, 'This is what global warming looks like.' A light snowfall... Greta, stay warm. In fact, you should turn off the heat. Don't be concerned! We're afraid we can't suggest it right now...

The year 2020 marks the start of a new solar cycle, which might be the weakest in at least 200 years, resembling the Little Ice Age. Even in Florida, the temperature is just 10 degrees. we would have had to go even further south due to global warming.'

'Lower level of living' as a result of 'anti-industry extremists'

'Climate change propaganda has become a huge economic issue damaging the global economy, decreasing the common person's level of living. Governments have adopted it solely because it is an excellent method of raising revenue.'

'This entire strategy has been put together by true zealots who are anti-Industrial Revolution.' Jennifer Morgan (Greenpeace, Greta's puppet master) and Al Gore have pushed through a very twisted theory based on unsubstantiated facts, such as the claim that there is 97 percent consensus (which is an outright lie, it's rather the opposite) and that the cyclical oscillation since the end of the Little Ice Age in the early 19th century is entirely due to humans, while refusing to look at the horde.

'The Eurozone is doomed,' says one expert.

'Their determination to impose their beliefs through more taxes and regulation (the EU's ridiculously costly 'Green Deal') has caused the German economy to collapse, destroying the whole Eurozone. Gore and Morgan have worked together to silence any opponents of their cause, despite the fact that they should be extensively examined. It's starting to seem like a witch hunt.'

'Even in hindsight, 2020 will appear to be a very significant turning point.' According to NASA, the weakest solar cycle in 200 years will peak in 2025. 'And if there is a sudden rise in volcanic eruptions (one of the symptoms of global cooling), then two or three 6+ eruptions might trigger a volcanic winter, which will significantly raise food costs.'

Is it still possible to avert Europe's economic and social suicide?

Future generations will wonder how the leaders of Europe's once-great civilization could lose their heads by making the ravings of a mentally disturbed teenage girl into law, and then commit economic and social suicide by demolishing their own prosperous industrial society, causing death and destruction on a historically unprecedented scale among their own people.

Unless we drastically alter our direction through the ballot box by no later than 2021. Is that still a possibility? Martin Armstrong has already given up hope, believing that we would have to go through a protracted and unprecedented catastrophe to rid our society of the dominant green Marxist climate doctrine, and then maybe rebuild a better world on the wreckage left by left-liberal globalists.

Donald Trump: We must reject doomsayers and remain hopeful.

However, at Davos, one world leader is striking a healthy dissenting note: US President Donald Trump. 'This is not the moment for pessimism, but rather for hope... To embrace tomorrow's possibilities, we must reject the endless prophets of doom and their predictions of a (climate) catastrophe... They want us to fail, but we are not going to allow that to happen. They projected overcrowding in the 1960s, mass death in the 1970s, and the end of oil in the 1990s.'

'These alarmists desire the same thing every time: full authority to dominate, modify, and control every element of our life.' But we will never let extreme socialists destroy our economy, damage our country, or annihilate our freedom. America will always be a proud, powerful, and unwavering stronghold of liberty.'

Chapter 10: The new and deadly green deal?

Ocasio-'Green Cortez's New Deal' entails 'the extinction of all life on Earth' - 'If fossil fuels are abolished, every tree on the planet will be chopped down.'

Dr. Patrick Moore, co-founder of Greenpeace, has slammed Alexandria Ocasio-Cortez (picture), the new darling of America's 'progressive' left. The 'Democratic Socialist' has proposed a 'Green New Deal,' which would cost tens of billions of dollars and, according to many detractors, will return the United States to pre-industrial civilization. Moore called Ocasio-Cortez a "hypocrite" and a "pompous dork" because executing her demand to phase out fossil fuels—which the European administration has already begun to do with the natural gas shutdown—will result in "mass fatalities."

Moore quit "his" Greenpeace years ago when the environmental organization was hijacked from within by far-left anarchists like Ocasio-Cortez.

All flights and automobiles must be grounded (except for her own)

The "Green New Deal" proposes that the United States abandon all reliance on oil, gas, and nuclear power. Trains must replace air transport (even across seas), and 99 percent of all automobiles must be phased out.

64

Of course, with the exception of the governing class, things went on as normal. According to the New York Post, Ocasio has a massive "carbon footprint," in part because her campaign staff relies nearly entirely on normal gasoline automobiles. She flew 66 times between May 2017 and December of last year, compared to only 18 times by rail, which, if she had her way, everyone would be obliged to convert to.

Socialist funds continue to push for free housing.

Furthermore, every structure in the United States will have to be extensively changed or possibly rebuilt to fulfill extremely stringent climatic regulations. Cortez proposes funding for millions of government positions for this reason. Those who do not wish to work will, by the way, be free to stay at home and will no longer be required to pay housing costs. But who would desire that?

How does "AOC" intend to fund its green utopia? Simply put, the only way to pay its draconian and enormously expensive plans is to turn on the money presses. Because 'we are going to get it right this time,' Cortez stated in an earlier interview, the fact that this socialism has resulted in widespread poverty and misery throughout history should not be a concern.

'This plan entails the annihilation of all life.' Brilliant'

According to the Green New Deal, all greenhouse emissions must be eliminated from the environment. Moore's response: 'Technically (scientifically) speaking, this implies deleting all water vapor and all CO2, which implies eradicating all life.' Brilliant.'

'If you don't like the deal, you should just come up with your own bold proposal to tackle the global climate catastrophe,' AOC tweeted later. Until then, we're in command, and you're simply yelling from the stands.'

The depletion of fossil fuels will result in mass deaths.'

Moore retorted, 'pompous dork.' You have no strategy to feed 8 billion people without using fossil fuels, or to deliver food into cities. Horses? If fossil fuels are outlawed, every tree on the planet will be felled in order to provide fuel for cooking and heating. You will kill a lot of people... You are nothing more than a hypocrite like the rest of them, with ZERO competence in any field you claim to be knowledgeable in.'

'You are suffering from illusions if you think fossil fuels will disappear anytime soon,' Moore added later in response to a tweet from another climate zealot who said that 'the end of fossil fuels is certain.' Perhaps in 500 years. The attitude of AOC is reckless and insulting. She is a newbie who pretends to be intelligent. If her sort is in command, she will wreck us.'

Our other books

Check out our other books for other unreported news, exposed facts and debunked truths, and more.

Join the exclusive Rebel Press Media Circle!

You will get a new updates about the unreported reality delivered in your inbox every Friday.

Sign up here today:

https://campsite.bio/rebelpressmedia

CPSIA information can be obtained
at www.ICGtesting.com
Printed in the USA
BVHW041024060322
630755BV00018B/2398